W9-AYO-691

Poetry Builders

Ana and Adam Build an
ACROSTIC

by Victoria Peterson-Hilleque
illustrated by Winifred Barnum-Newman

Content Consultant
Kris Bigalk
Director of Creative Writing
Normandale Community College

NORWOOD HOUSE PRESS
CHICAGO, ILLINOIS

J808.1
PET

Norwood House Press
P.O. Box 316598
Chicago, Illinois 60631
For information regarding Norwood House Press, please visit our website at:
www.norwoodhousepress.com or call 866-565-2900.

Editor: Melissa York
Designer: Emily Love
Project Management: Red Line Editorial

Library of Congress Cataloging-in-Publication Data
Peterson-Hilleque, Victoria, 1971-
  Ana and Adam build an acrostic / by Victoria Peterson-Hilleque ; illustrated by Winifred Barnum-Newman.
      p. cm. -- (Poetry builders)
  Includes bibliographical references.
  Summary: "Ana and Adam learn concepts related to writing acrostics as they read and write coded messages. Includes creative writing exercises to assist the reader in writing acrostic poems"--Provided by publisher.
  ISBN-13: 978-1-59953-433-6 (library ed. : alk. paper)
  ISBN-10: 1-59953-433-9 (library ed. : alk. paper)
  1. Acrostics--Authorship--Juvenile literature. 2. Acrostics--Authorship--Juvenile fiction. I. Newman, Winifred Barnum, ill. II. Title.
  PN1525.P47 2011
  808.1--dc22
                              2010043211

©2011 by Norwood House Press.
All rights reserved.
No part of this book may be reproduced without written permission from the publisher.
Manufactured in the United States of America in North Mankato, Minnesota.
169N—012011

Words in **black bold** are defined in the glossary.

"Why I Like Poetry"

I never thought I'd say this, but I like poetry!
I used to think poetry was for old people
who never go outside. I thought that since I
liked poetry I should keep it a secret. That's
not true!

Honestly, I did not like reading or writing
at all until last year. Then I started reading
comic books and got into reading and
writing about everything, including poetry.

My favorite kind of poetry is acrostic poetry.
An acrostic poem starts with a word. You
write the word up and down, so there's just
one letter on each line. Then you fill in the
lines. This poem I wrote spells acrostic.

A poem with a
Clue on every line
Read down
Only first letters
Soon you'll discover
The mystery word
It's like a secret
Code!

By Adam, age 10

Plit . . . Plit . . . Plit.

What was that noise?

Plit-plit-plit-plit-plit.

Ana turned to see little cereal pieces bouncing off her window.

"Adam!" she called, opening her window. She saw her best friend leaning out of his own bedroom window across the alley.

"Shhhhhh!" Adam hissed. "I mean, be quiet, please. Here—" He tossed her a balled-up paper.

"Caught it!" Ana hissed back. She smoothed
open the note.

This note is for your eyes
Only!
Put everything down at once.
Sneak over for an
Emergency meeting at the
Clubhouse to
Read
Extremely interesting
Things!

Ana grabbed her secret spy notebook and
took off.

7

"Did anyone see you?" Adam asked Ana as she crawled inside the clubhouse.

"I don't think so," Ana said. She plopped down next to Adam. "Is this one of those poems Mr. Buxton was telling us about? An A-something?"

"Yeah, acrostic," Adam said.

Ana peered at the note again. She ran her finger along the first letter of every line. "T-O-P S-E-C-R-E-T. It spells TOP SECRET!"

"It spells TOP SECRET and it is top secret," Adam said.

"Check this out," he said, pulling out a pink notebook from behind his back. "I found it in the bottom of a closet," he explained.

"Wow, this looks old!" Ana exclaimed.

"It's my mom's, from when she was in high school," Adam said, turning to a page.

Kenny,
I remember the
Starry night
Start of
Me and you
Everlasting love

"Kenny?—That's your dad!" Ana said. She ran her finger along the left side of the poem. "Wait a minute. This poem is an acrostic. It spells—"

"KISS ME!" Adam gasped.

"EEEEEwwww!" the two friends yelled.

"Look at this one." Adam turned the page.

Disgusting
Annoying
Rude
Rarely mature
Yucky hair
Loves to bug me

"Darryl is my mom's brother. My uncle Darryl," Adam explained.

"Wow," Ana said, "and I thought my brother Stewart and I fought a lot. My mom's always telling us to be nicer to each other."

"Same with my sister, Gloria," Adam added.

Adam leaned back on a giant pillow and stared at the ceiling. "Mom and Uncle Darryl are good friends now, though. Weird."

"I know," Ana said. "Do you think you and Gloria will be like that some day?"

"I don't know," Adam said slowly. "Maybe."

Ana leaned back on the pillow next to Adam. She squinted at the Christmas lights to make them look like stars.

"Ana?" Adam said.

"Yeah?" Ana blinked fast to make the stars twinkle.

"What would you write if you were going to do an acrostic about Stewart?"

"I don't know. What would you say about Gloria?"

"I don't know." Adam shrugged. "You want to try?"

"Sure," Ana said. She sat up and ripped a page out of her notebook for Adam. Adam wrote G-L-O-R-I-A down his page; Ana wrote S-T-E-W-A-R-T.

They started to fill in the lines. Then Ana sighed, ripped her paper out of her notebook and crumpled it up. "I can't think of a good R-word for the R-line."

"All I have for G is giant, and that doesn't make any sense," Adam added. "Let's just forget about the letters for a minute. We're supposed to start by **free writing**, anyway. That's what Mr. Buxton would say."

"To warm up the brain!" Ana said with one raised finger, doing her best to imitate their fourth grade teacher. "List everything you can think of about your sister," she continued in her deepest voice, "how she looks and smells, what you do together, how she makes you feel. Write everything that enters your mind. Don't worry about **form** yet. You can **revise** later."

"Yes, sir, Mr. Buxton!" Adam said.

That made Ana snort. "Ready, set, go!" she said, and the two friends got to work.

When they were done they showed each
other their lists.

Adam:

Gloria is
a neat freak
loves to dance
rides a red bike
spends most of her money on clothes
loves spy stories like me (but pretends she doesn't)
practices piano every day without being told
likes to do puzzles with me
likes fishing with me at our family cabin

Ana:

Stewart
smells like peanut butter
wears hi-tops that smell like sweaty feet
also wears skinny black jeans with a leather
jacket a lot!
has an iguana
keeps his old Pokémon cards
keeps notes from his old girlfriend, Ashley, in
a shoebox in his closet
still builds stuff with me with my Legos

practices piano

puzzles

red bike

Fishing

neat freak

dancing

loves spy sTories

"I still don't have a good R-word," Ana said.

"What about, instead of *smells like peanut butter,* you said *really loves peanut butter*?" Adam asked.

"I don't know." Ana sounded disappointed. She stared at her list for a while. "Wait a minute—*reeks like peanut butter* might work."

has an iguana

legos

peanut butter

skinny black pants

leather jacket

smelly feet

high tops

The two friends worked by themselves for several minutes. Sometimes Adam had to stare at the ceiling more, and Ana stopped to squint at the lights. Pink eraser dust was everywhere.

When they were done, they showed each other their poems. Adam went first.

Grins
Luring in the fish
On her line.
Reeling so slowly
Is fun to be with
At the cabin.

"Cool!" Ana said.

"I liked thinking about fishing at the cabin," Adam explained.

"I know what you mean," Ana said. "I liked thinking about Legos. I didn't even use *reeks like peanut butter.* Take a look."

Still builds
Towers with Legos, and
Eight kinds of spaceships, and
Weird
Aliens and creepy
Robots
Too bad he stinks.

"Ha!" Adam laughed. "Remember that time you guys tried to make that Lego T-rex but it looked more like a cactus?"

"Aha!" Ana said. She crossed out *towers* and wrote *T-rex* instead. "We don't even really make towers," she explained. "I just couldn't think of anything else. But now, it's perfect. . . . Want to try writing about each other?"

"Definitely," Adam said. "I have an idea for A already—Awesome at acrostics!"

You Can Write an Acrostic Poem, too!

Acrostic poems spell a word or phrase with the first letter of each line. Lines can be long or short. There are as many lines as there are letters in the secret word or phrase.

You can write your acrostic using someone's name or using any word you want. You can write long acrostic poems with more than one word, too. Making lists can help you get started.

Maybe you love winter. What do you like about the season? What words or phrases describe winter to you?

snow so deep, sparkling, sunshine, bright, white, cold, crisp, gasp, cloudy breath, slipping and sliding on ice, building a snowman, hiding in a fort and throwing snowballs, staying home from school for a snow day

Do not worry about the form right away. Just let yourself write freely.

Once you have a lot of ideas, write your word or phrase down on your notebook page and experiment with your notes. Try different combinations. Try reading your poems out loud to yourself or a friend. When you're ready, you can put it all together.

Snow a mile deep—
No school today!
Outside in the white crisp sparkling sunshine,
We fight a battle with snow.

Dusk comes early in the winter.
All I want is one more hour because I'm not ready to come in
Yet.

Glossary

form: the rules your poem follows.

free writing: writing whatever comes to mind about a subject without going back to change anything.

revise: to make changes to your poem.

For More Information

Books

Harley, Avis. *African Acrostics: A Word in Edgeways*. Somerville, MA: Candlewick Press, 2009.

Prelutsky, Jack. *Pizza, Pigs, and Poetry: How to Write a Poem*. New York: Greenwillow Books, 2008.

Schnur, Steven. *Winter: An Alphabet Acrostic*. New York: Clarion Books, 2002.

Websites

Giggle Poetry: How to Write Acrostic Poems
http://www.gigglepoetry.com/poetryclass/acrostic.html
Children's poet Bruce Lansky explains how to write acrostic poems.

Read Write Think: Acrostic Poems
http://www.readwritethink.org/files/resources/interactives/acrostic/
This interactive website guides you in writing your own acrostic poems.

About the Author

Victoria Peterson-Hilleque lives with her family in Minneapolis, Minnesota. She has a master's degree in English literature from the University of St. Thomas and a master's of fine arts in poetry from Hamline University.

About the Illustrator

Winifred Barnum-Newman is a painter, sculptor, and designer.